W9-BXL-581

CELEBRATING OUR COMMUNITIES

CELEBRATING ALL APPEARANCES

BY ABBY COLICH

BLUE OWL
BOOKS

TIPS FOR CAREGIVERS

Social and emotional learning (SEL) helps children manage emotions, learn how to feel empathy, create and achieve goals, and make good decisions. Strong lessons and support in SEL will help children establish positive habits in communication, cooperation, and decision-making. By incorporating SEL in early reading, children will learn the importance of accepting and celebrating all people in their communities.

BEFORE READING

Talk to the reader about appearances. Explain that appearance has to do with how someone looks and that everyone looks different.

Discuss: How would you describe what you look like? Why do you think people look the way they do? What are some ways that people look different from one another?

AFTER READING

Talk to the reader about ways he or she can celebrate differences with others.

Discuss: What is one way you can accept another person's appearance? Why should we be accepting of others? Why is it good for a community to celebrate all people?

SEL GOAL

Children may have a loose understanding of acceptance. They have likely heard to not make fun of or exclude others for being different, but they may not understand why. Talk to readers about the importance of empathy in accepting and celebrating the differences of others. Ask them to imagine what it feels like to be singled out for being different or made fun of for their looks. Make a list of these different feelings. Then ask readers to list the feelings they have when they are included and accepted. Explain that our communities are better when everyone is accepted and included.

TABLE OF CONTENTS

CHAPTER 1

A LOOK AT APPEARANCE

Are you short or tall? Do you have straight or curly hair? Each of us has our own **appearance**. This is the way we look. Height, weight, and skin and hair color are just a few things that make up your appearance.

Why do we look the way we do? One reason is **genes**. Genes are in the **cells** that make up your body. They hold the information that make you who you are. They are passed on from your parents. Do you have the same hair and eye color as your mom or dad?

Some looks we choose. How we **style** our hair or the clothes we wear are part of our appearance. Everyone in a **community** has his or her own appearance.

YOUR STYLE

What do you like to wear? How do you like to style your hair? These choices can be fun ways to **express** yourself and your interests! It's important to respect others who do the same.

There is so much more to a person than how he or she looks! Everyone has strengths. And we can accomplish more together. Communities are stronger when we **accept** and include everyone.

Ted is a great artist. Ann has neat handwriting. Together, they make a book!

CHAPTER 2

IT STARTS WITH YOU

Do you wish you weren't so tall? Find the positive! You are great at basketball. Make a list. What else are you good at? What makes you feel good?

My Strengths

1. Basketball
2.
3.
4.
5.

When you think about your strengths, you begin to accept your whole self. Accepting yourself feels good! And it will help you accept others. When we look past appearances, we can begin to really see and understand others.

One way to accept and get to know others is to show respect. When you respect people, you show that you care about how they feel. You are nice and treat them with kindness. Looks don't matter.

Aiden is a new neighbor. He uses a wheelchair. You see him playing alone outside. You invite him to play a game!

GOLDEN RULE

Have you heard the saying, "Treat others as you want to be treated"? This is the Golden Rule. You want to be respected and treated equally, so you should do the same!

Mia is teased for wearing glasses. Try to think about and understand how she feels. Ask her. This is called **empathy**. Learning and showing empathy can be hard. But it will help you understand, respect, and accept others. They will feel accepted, too.

Jonah and Jack are different **races**. Jonah asks Jack questions about his life. He gets to know him and finds out they have a lot in common. They both love olives on pizza, and they both love soccer. Jack and Jonah are more alike than they thought!

Set a good example for others. Ivy is left out because she dresses differently. Mariah invites her to play. They plan a day to dress the same. Other kids at school see that Mariah accepts everyone. They may want to do the same.

WHAT TO SAY

Are people making fun of someone's looks? Try saying, "Hey, that's not nice," and then change the subject. Not sure how to start talking to someone for the first time? Ask what book he or she last read or what they like to do after school.

CHAPTER 3

CELEBRATE DIFFERENCES

Everyone looks different. But looks are just one part of what makes people who they are.

Everyone is good at something. When we work together, our communities are stronger, and we can accomplish more. What strengths do you bring to your community?

Disaster Relief

GOALS AND TOOLS

GROW WITH GOALS

Accepting all people, no matter what they look like, is important. Focusing on people's other qualities will help you be more accepting.

Goal: Name some things that are more important than how someone looks. Why should you remember these things when getting to know someone?

Goal: Think of a time you felt empathy toward someone. If you can't think of anything, try to find a time when you can. Do you see someone who looks sad? Ask that person how he or she feels and why.

Goal: Get to know someone you haven't spoken with much before. Try to find one thing you have in common or both like.

WRITING REFLECTION

Accepting yourself can help you be more accepting of those around you.

1. What is one thing you are good at or something you like about yourself?

2. What is one thing about yourself you wish you could change?

3. What is one thing you can do to be more accepting of others?

GLOSSARY

accept
To agree that something is correct, satisfactory, or enough.

appearance
The way something or someone looks.

cells
The smallest units of a human, plant, or animal.

community
A group of people who all have something in common.

empathy
The ability to understand, be sensitive to, and care about the feelings of others.

express
To show what you feel or think with words, writing, or actions.

genes
The parts that make up your body's chromosomes. Genes are passed from parents to children and determine how you look and the way you grow.

races
The major groups into which human beings can be divided. People of the same race have similar physical characteristics, such as skin color, which are passed on from one generation to the next.

style
To give a shape to a person's hair.

TO LEARN MORE

Finding more information is as easy as 1, 2, 3.

1. Go to www.factsurfer.com

2. Enter "**celebratingallappearances**" into the search box.

3. Choose your cover to see a list of websites.

INDEX

Blue Owl Books are published by Jump!, 5357 Penn Avenue South, Minneapolis, MN 55419, www.jumplibrary.com

Copyright © 2021 Jump! International copyright reserved in all countries. No part of this book may be reproduced in any form without written permission from the publisher.

Library of Congress Cataloging-in-Publication Data

Names: Colich, Abby, author.
Title: Celebrating all appearances / by Abby Colich.
Description: Blue owl books. | Minneapolis, MN: Jump!, Inc., [2021]
Series: Celebrating our communities | Includes index.
Audience: Ages 7–10.
Identifiers: LCCN 2019043151 (print)
LCCN 2019043152 (ebook)
ISBN 9781645273622 (hardcover)
ISBN 9781645273639 (paperback)
ISBN 9781645273646 (ebook)
Subjects: LCSH: Physical-appearance-based bias–Juvenile literature. | Prejudices–Juvenile literature. | Toleration–Juvenile literature.
Classification: LCC HM1091 .C6425 2021 (print) | LCC HM1091 (ebook) | DDC 303.3/85–dc23
LC record available at https://lccn.loc.gov/2019043151
LC ebook record available at https://lccn.loc.gov/2019043152

Editor: Jenna Gleisner
Designer: Michelle Sonnek

Photo Credits: ranplett/iStock, cover; FatCamera/iStock, 1; Pixel-Shot/Shutterstock, 3 (left); Djomas/Shutterstock, 3 (right); gradyreese/iStock, 4; Deepak Sethi/iStock, 5; Zurijeta/Shutterstock, 6–7; kali9/iStock, 8–9; photastic/Shutterstock, 10; Asier Romero/Shutterstock, 11; Richard Hutchings/Getty, 12–13; Gelpi/Shutterstock, 14–15; LightField Studios/Shutterstock, 16–17; Just dance/Shutterstock, 18–19; JohnnyGreig/iStock, 20; fstop123/iStock, 21.

Printed in the United States of America at Corporate Graphics in North Mankato, Minnesota.